P9-EAY-146

Table of Contents

DAVID O. MCKAY LIBRARY

3 1404 00883 1197

Librarians
Ready, Dee AR 2.5 LG

FEB 8 2011

DATE DUE

MAR 2 7 2015 2011		
MAR 2 7 2015		
APR 2 0 2015		
JUL 1 5 2015		

Demco

WITHDRAWN

PROPERTY OF:
D O. McKAY LIBRARY
BYU-IDAHO
XBURG ID 83460-0405

MARY 8

DAVID O. McKAY LIBRARY
BYU-IDAHO

Community Helpers

Librarians

by Dee Ready

Content Consultants:
Kathleen Baxter, Supervisor of Youth Services
Anoka County (Minn.) Library
Gretchen Wronka, Youth Services Coordinator
Hennepin County (Minn.) Library

Bridgestone Books

an imprint of Capstone Press

Bridgestone Books are published by Capstone Press
151 Good Counsel Drive, P.O. Box 669, Mankato, Minnesota 56002
www.capstonepress.com

Copyright © 1998 by Capstone Press. All rights reserved.
No part of this publication may be reproduced in whole or in part, or stored in a retrieval
system, or transmitted in any form or by any means, electronic, mechanical, photocopying,
recording, or otherwise, without written permission of the publisher.
For information regarding permission, write to Capstone Press,
151 Good Counsel Drive, P.O. Box 669, Dept. R, Mankato, Minnesota 56002.
Printed in the United States of America

Library of Congress Cataloging-in-Publication Data
Ready, Dee.
    Librarians/by Dee Ready.
    p. cm.—(Community helpers)
    Includes bibliographical references and index.
    Summary: Explains the tools, schooling, and work of librarians.
    ISBN-13: 978-1-56065-559-6 (hardcover)   ISBN-10: 1-56065-559-3 (hardcover)
    ISBN-13: 978-0-7368-8456-3 (softcover pbk.)   ISBN-10: 0-7368-8456-4 (softcover pbk.)
    1. Library science—United States—Juvenile literature. 2. Librarians—United
States—Juvenile literature. [1. Librarians. 2. Occupations.] I. Title. II. Series:
Community helpers (Mankato, Minn.)
Z665.5.R43   1998
023'.2--dc21   97-2972
                          CIP
                          AC

Editorial credits
Editor, Timothy Larson; Cover design, Timothy Halldin
Photo research assistant, Michelle Norstad

Photo credits
International Stock/George Ancona, 6; Ronn Maratea, cover, 10
Maguire PhotoGraFX, 12
Unicorn Stock/Jeff Greenberg, 4, 8, 16; Karen Holsinger Mullen, 14;
  Martha McBride, 18; Martin R. Jones, 20

2 3 4 5 6 06 05 04 03 02

Librarians

Librarians use libraries to help people learn. A library is a place where people can find information. Information is facts and ideas. Librarians help people find information in books and on computers.

What Librarians Do

Librarians teach people how to find answers to questions. Librarians look for new books and other items for the library. Items are things like videos and newspapers. Librarians also help people find books to read for fun. They read stories to groups of people, too.

Where Librarians Work

Librarians work in libraries. Libraries have shelves filled with books and newspapers. Libraries have videos and music. People can borrow these items. Libraries have computers for people to use, too.

Different Kinds of Librarians

Many librarians work in public libraries or in school libraries. Other librarians work in special libraries. These libraries may be in law offices or work places. They also may be in hospitals or other places.

Tools Librarians Use

Librarians use computer catalogs. These catalogs list everything in a library. They show librarians where items can be found. Librarians also use computers to look for other information. They use charts and maps. They use books and other tools, too.

Librarians and Communities

Some librarians work on bookmobiles. A bookmobile is a special van or truck. It has many of the same items found in a library. Librarians use bookmobiles to help people who cannot come to libraries. People can borrow library items from bookmobiles.

Librarians and School

People go to college to become librarians. College is where people study after high school. They learn about libraries. They learn how to find information. Some librarians go to college for six or more years.

People Who Help Librarians

Library aides help librarians. They help people find items in the library. They check out books and other items to people. Library aides also put items on library shelves. They mend old books, too.

Librarians Help Others

Librarians help people learn. They help people find information. They help people find answers to questions. Librarians help people see that learning is fun.

Hands On: Hold Your Own Storytime

Librarians read stories to people. They read stories to groups of people during storytimes.

You can hold your own storytime for your friends and family.

1. Pick out a book or a few books you like. Read through them to make sure you know the words.
2. Pick a time for your storytime. Pick a place to hold your storytime. The time and place are up to you.
3. Set up chairs for people to sit on. You can also have them sit on blankets or pillows.
4. Ask your friends and family to come to your storytime. Make sure they know the time and place.
5. Have your friends and family sit down. Read your stories. Show the people any pictures on the pages as you read. Answer questions people might have.

Words to Know

bookmobile (BUK-moh-beel)—a van or truck that has library books and other things

computer catalog (kuhm-PYOO-tur KAT-uh-log)—a special list of all the things in a library and where they can be found

college (KOL-ij)—a school where people study after high school

information (in-fur-MAY-shuhn)—facts and ideas

items (EYE-tuhms)—things like videos and newspapers

library (LYE-brer-ee)—a place where people can find information

Read More

Burby, Liza N. *A Day in the Life of a Librarian.* New York: PowerKids Press, 1999.

Greene, Carol. *Librarians Help Us Find Information.* Chanhassen, Minn.: Child's World, 1999.

Internet Sites

The Internet Public Library
http://www.ipl.org
Kids Web Digital Library
http://www.kidsvista.com/index.html

Index